Elementary EDUC 101:
What They Didn't Teach You in College

By: Gretchen E. Bridgers

Elementary EDUC 101: What They Didn't Teach You in College
By: Gretchen E. Bridgers

ISBN: 978-1-7330949-0-0

Library of Congress Control Number: 2019911700

Editor: Dana Hopkins
Cover Designer: Prudence of Books Will $ell

Published by Always A Lesson, LLC.

Printed in the United States of America.

First printing edition September 4, 2014.

Always A Lesson, LLC
2101 Blueberry Street
Belmont, NC 28012

www.alwaysalesson.com

Dedication

I dedicate this book to my five nephews (Devin, Jack, Luke, Owen and Ian) as well as to my two daughters (Lily and Avery).

They inspire me to help educators become not only better teachers but impactful leaders so all children can successfully reach their potential.

I love you and know each of you will become your very best as you grow and learn in school and life. DREAM BIG!

Forward

Every year, schools in the US hire more than 200,000 new teachers for that first day of class. Those who make it beyond the first year won't stay long: about 30 percent of new teachers leave the profession after just three years and more than 50 percent after five. These statistics are mind-blowing and yet in this country alone we still struggle to keep our new teachers for the long haul. What can we do to support new teachers in a way that will encourage them to stay? What supports can we offer to bridge the gap between what new teachers have learned from their University pre-service programs to the work they're actually going to encounter when they finally make it to the classroom?

As someone who has spent over 25 years working in the public school system as a teacher, principal, education consultant and now a school board member one thing is clear: all teachers need a strong support system, especially those who are just starting their teaching journey. We know that those new to the profession need the opportunity of mentoring and even a safety net in order to be able to be successful in their work. When new teachers lack those supportive tools the fear of failure can cause them to leave the teaching profession before they've had time to establish a strong foundation for themselves.

With all the information that new teachers need to absorb as they start out, the overwhelm can cause them to feel isolated or disconnected. With the wide variety of books, social media tools, and professional learning communities there is no reason for new teachers to feel alone, isolated, or at a loss for knowing what to do in any situation.

Creating a resource for new teachers can be challenging but through her book filled with easy to implement tips, ideas, and strategies, Gretchen has provided a tool kit which will serve as a support to new teachers. It will help them to build confidence in harnessing easily accessible resources that she provides so that they can be more successful. Each chapter includes a practical list of tips and suggestions that a new teacher can easily follow.

In each chapter, Gretchen delivers step-by-step practical applications that a new teacher can use as they are getting started in their first classroom. Her book serves as a guide to help both new teachers, and anyone working with new teachers, to mobilize the power of key strategies to mentor and empower new teachers to make informed decisions, design their classroom, build relationships and connect to the most important stakeholders in education: the students!

Much of the real power of Gretchen's book comes from her sharing real-life experiences and tips for successful implementation which will provide those building blocks of support that any new teacher can appreciate.

As an advocate and mentor of new teachers, I hope you will see the value of adding this book to your arsenal of teaching resources!

- *Lisa Michelle Dabbs*
  Author of Standing in the Gap: Empowering New Teachers Through Connected Resources

Before I ever became a teacher, my heart was already hooked on teaching others. Ms. Lofy, my fourth grade teacher at St. Isidore's School in Danville, California, inspired my love for teaching. She made learning fun, and she seemed to have fun doing it. I loved learning, and observing my teacher intrigued me. I wished I could correct papers, see answers in the textbook, and write out report cards. It sounds silly that those things seemed fun to me, but they really did! I played teacher in my parents' living room by passing out papers and instructing imaginary students. I even had my parents sit in class a few times. Boy, was my dad unruly as he flirted with my mom and copied all of her answers! I continued this imaginative play for much of my childhood.

When it came time to select the perfect college, I was perplexed. I knew what I wanted to become but had no clue how to get there. My eye was on the prize, and mentally I was already at my destination. In High School, my mother had to set the timer and make me choose between two schools. I was indifferent to where I was going, because in my mind I was already a teacher. I hated my college teaching courses because I had to memorize educational terms and learn about the great educators who came before us. It was important, I guess, but not how I wanted to be spending my time. I wanted to jump in. Luckily, my college placed teachers into classrooms as early as freshman year to observe. This was my favorite part of the day because I could really imagine myself being a teacher. I walked in teachers' classrooms, noticing every detail and mentally jotting down ideas.

I loved building relationships with the students. By the time my student teaching placement occurred, I was ready to teach full time. Much to my dismay, that was not allowed. I had to go through the motions with gradual submersion. Those who observed me said I was "a natural." I was on fire with excitement and motivation. I began reading books geared toward the educational field to gain knowledge and insight into the life of a teacher. As my love for teaching grew, I began to record ideas I would hear or read about on note cards in a recipe box, anything from cute bulletin boards and festive art projects to classroom management strategies. By the end of college, my index card box was full!

Before I landed my first real job, I looked over each index card and decided what techniques I was going to implement and what I might save for a later date. (I already had the job in my mind, remember?) I taught for five years in an elementary school with a high economically disadvantaged population. Through my experience, I added more index cards to my recipe box.

I went on to receive my master's degree. The courses were theory-heavy with limited application. I was back to daydreaming about my note cards and making my classroom the best learning environment for my students. I was proud that I knew I was on the right path to gaining knowledge, but it was not satisfying my hunger for revolutionizing my own teaching practice.

Still seeking growth and knowledge, I continued my own education and delved deep into the National Board process. I learned so much about myself as a teacher as I wrote lessons, filmed my delivery of the content, and wrote reflections not only on how I did as an instructor but also on how my students did as learners. This allowed me to see myself from another point of view. I was able to evaluate my own craft and become better through my self-reflection and analysis of student work. I learned more in this process than during my entire college career because it was relevant and applicable in the moment, and I saw the benefits immediately. (I am so passionate about this milestone in my journey that I encourage all educators to go through the process. You are doing yourself and your students the biggest favor by becoming your best!)

I then transitioned my work into a suburban school, which was very different from my first school in terms of student background, needs, and performance levels. This change in student population continued to help me grow as a teacher of *all* children. I added great ideas to my index card box daily.

The next part of my journey is my career favorite-to-date: training new teachers. This allowed me to look back at all I had accomplished and know that I truly had arrived to where I always saw myself—I am a teacher, a good teacher. It was now time to be *great* by helping other teachers on their journey. It is like I reached my own finish line and now I am taking another lap with a buddy to mentor along the route. I had been a cooperating teacher for student teachers, mentored new teachers in the building, helped revamp our new teacher support program and even joined forces with a local program to get great teachers into the neediest schools in the district by providing personalized and thorough coaching. I worked after hours and during summer school sessions with TEACH Charlotte of The New Teacher Project [TNTP] in various roles—admitting adults into the program, instructing them on effective teaching techniques, and coaching them during their student teaching placement in the classroom as they implemented the techniques outlined in the book *Teach Like a Champion* by Doug Lemov. This was so rewarding for me because I saw myself in those teachers-to-be. I remembered the thoughts and questions that ran through my own head. I tried to answer as many of those things early on before candidates even realized that they might want to ask me something.

During this time, I started a blog called Always A Lesson to share my journey in the classroom with other teachers. Whether I was teaching a lesson or learning one myself, the blog was the perfect place to record my thoughts. There is always a lesson we can learn from our experiences. It was an outlet for my teaching reflections, but it allowed me to connect with other edu-bloggers in the world. Eventually that blog turned into a full website, featuring a blog, podcast, webinars, and classroom resources for teachers. The information I share on my website is a compilation of my personal experience in the classroom as a teacher and a teacher leader as well as instructional best practices I have acquired through my connections with top notch educators on social media.

Throughout my teaching and leading experience, I have realized that those who are going to become teachers still need to know things that are not taught in traditional degree courses. During those first few years of teaching, I kept finding myself saying, "Gosh, if I had only known that *before* I started teaching!" or "Why did no one tell me it was like *this*?" As my teaching years wore on, I realized someone *does* need to tell future educators what it is really like working on a school campus. College does a great job of teaching educational theory through the acts of numerous influential educators in our history. However, it does not focus a lot on real-world applications (of course, the quick student teaching stint is supposed to take care of that). There are so many questions a new teacher wonders daily, and this book will help sort out some of those unknowns. It focuses on the logistical aspects of teaching that first year instead of providing a book chock-full of fun ideas that you might not get to because your foundation for excellence was not set. But who knows, maybe in my next book I will publish my numerous index cards full of ideas!

I have always wanted to write a book. I knew the topic would relate to the educational field but was not sure exactly what it would look like. I am an avid reader recreationally as well as professionally. There is a lot of literature out there for educators, but not a lot for those who want and are ready to become educators. So, I began thinking about the topics I would want to read about as a beginning teacher. My list turned into a few pages and eventually this book. After a decade in K-12 classrooms, I decided to update the original version of this book with even more of my best tips and tricks for new teachers. I hope you truly enjoy it!

Please know that this book is based solely on *my* perspective, experience and opinion as an elementary school teacher in the United States. I encourage you to highlight and mark up this book as you make it part of your journey as an educator. If there is something in here you like, write it down on an index card and start your own collection! I hope this book acts as a springboard for many educators out there to discuss its contents and add on with their own tidbits. We must equip our teachers with the knowledge we have acquired throughout our own teaching experiences—pay it forward!

Table of Contents

1
Preparing to Become a Teacher

I am so excited you are thinking about becoming a teacher! An educator is so much more than an individual who stands in front of a classroom handing out worksheets and grading papers. The privilege of being a teacher is having the opportunity to affect change in the world right now by inspiring the young minds who will become our future leaders. Many students are bright but need moral guidance. Some students have the best manners but need more academic attention to shine. But all students need an adult who cares for them and loves them like his or her own. They deserve a teacher who will go to any length to ensure the child is successful and proud of their accomplishments—large or small. This profession makes all other professions possible and has a long-lasting impact on a child's self-esteem and cherished childhood memories. As a teacher, you get to be the hero who helps students develop into future entrepreneurs, presidents, service men and women. What an honor!

In an effort to best prepare yourself for the learning journey ahead, apply these three tips:

Stay connected. Chase your dream hard, network with current educators, and stay connected to children in any way possible—sports camps, tutoring, babysitting, etc. Follow and interact with inspiring educators on social media, especially in Twitter chats.

Get out there and dive into the educational field as much as possible until you achieve certification.

Stay educated. Read, read, read! Keep up-to-date on what techniques are working and failing in today's schools. Do not sit back and think you'll become a rock star teacher through osmosis. Some preparatory classes can be dry and encourage a daydream here and there, but I promise you, it's in your best interest to keep focused on the goal of leaving your imprint on future generations of children. Teaching is not a job, it's a lifestyle. You are only going to be as good as the amount of effort you put in. As a lifelong learner, you might master one technique but have another one waiting for you to tackle. You are never "finished." You are never "done." You teach children how to learn by modeling your own learning.

Take detailed notes. During your course instruction for educator preparation programs, take detailed notes. I looked back through these my first couple of years. Be sure to keep these notes in a binder with categorized tabs so it is easy to add information later on (i.e., classroom organization, classroom management, grading, etc.).

2
Landing the Job

First of all, *congratulations* on achieving your teacher certification! We need great teachers, and I have confidence that if you are reading this book, you will become one in no time. Landing your first teaching job can provoke some healthy anxiety over whether you will put your best foot forward.

The suggestions listed below will set you apart from the rest of the competition.

Prepare a résumé. A résumé is a brag board and you want to shine! There are many websites out there that can help you format a professional-looking one. For education, a two-page résumé is the standard, but if you can fit it onto one (not including references), that is preferable. A resumé is a working document, which means it is constantly being updated. As you learn and grow as an educator, you can add and delete information based on your current needs. The tips listed below will help your résumé stand out from the crowd:
- Collaborate with educators you respect and use their guidance to showcase your accomplishments.
- Include certifications acquired or special skills needed in the employment section.
- Explain how you went above-and-beyond your required duties, as it is assumed that you performed all of your duties to maintain said job.

- Write short and to the point. First impressions are made quickly, and if your résumé is too long, full of spelling errors, or too "busy" with fonts, pictures, or wordiness, it will most likely get tossed in the trash. Be simple. Be concise.
- Prioritize your accomplishments so the best ones appear first, to catch the reader's eye. You want potential employers to be impressed and intrigued so that they will continue reading more about you. Make them *have* to hire you!
- Ensure your references are aware that you are including their information, so they can best prepare for a phone call. Choose someone who can really speak about your ability, not just your next-door neighbor who thinks you're "darling."
- *Proofread* your résumé. I sat in on an interviewing panel one year and a person on the committee circled each résumé error of potential candidates. Of course, the owners of those résumés were not hired. Lead with your best foot forward.

Research potential schools and principals. Doing your homework prior to an interview will ensure you make a well-informed decision about your future employment. You will be spending a lot of your time at the school under the tutelage of the principal, so you'll want to do your due diligence. Follow the tips listed below to help you find your ideal work home:

- When you know the area where you want to teach, create a list of all of the schools located there. Pay attention to the school type (private, public, charter, etc.), student population, achievement ratings, class and grade level size, available government funding, and any other relevant data you find helpful. Be sure to note anything that makes that school stand out in comparison to others you have found. Then, narrow down your list by prioritizing your top choices.

- Drive by those locations and take a close look at the surrounding neighborhoods to get a feel for the school environment. Ask yourself, "Can I see myself working here?" If you notice someone in the campus parking lot, don't be afraid to roll down the window and ask a few questions. That person's opinion could be helpful to you, or even get you an "in" for an interview with the principal.

- Use the internet, especially a school's website, to find information about your principal that could clue you in on his or her style and philosophy. Ask yourself, "Will I learn well under their leadership style?" or "Do I agree with their educational approach or philosophy?" This might alleviate future frustrations that could result if you do not see eye-to-eye when it comes learning strategies or curricular initiatives.

Rehearse interviewing scenarios. There are some great websites and blogs out there loaded with educational interview questions, including mine. Most principals do not ask you a lot of theory or questions about famous educators. They will instead focus on your personal teaching philosophy and how you put that into action in the classroom. A lot of interview questions are not so much about the question itself but *how* you go about answering it. It shows your creativity, critical thinking, and uniqueness. So, answer outside the box!

Follow the tips below to prepare for potential interview scenarios.

- Reflect on your experience in classrooms thus far and collaborate with educators who have seen you in action.
- Create a list of possible interview questions, script out your answers, and practice. Do not memorize your answers or begin a drawn-out speech. Do know the important points you want to hit and allow your personality to shine through.
- Practice in a mirror to ease nerves and pinpoint any repetitive gestures.
- Record yourself and listen for words you use often, use slow, articulate speech, and eliminate "ums" or "uhs"! Feel free to videotape yourself too. You want what you say to be powerful and not jumbled or ill-prepared.
- Don't forget to smile and have fun!

To help you get started, I have listed some popular interview questions below as well as included what the interviewer is really after when asking that question. (If you use my answers in an interview, I expect a shout-out—just kidding!)

- *What is the last book you read?*

This is another version of the most popular interview question: Tell me about yourself. Because that question is so broad and vague, it has started to morph into something more specific. Interviewers want to know your interests, but also wonder about your dedication to lifelong learning in your field. Be sure to state the book title, why you wanted to read it and what lesson or information you took away from it. Always bring it back to education, even if the book was not specifically geared towards education.

• *What do you admire about a leader?*

They want to see if you think big picture and reference such things as "supports me to gain knowledge and experience" or focus on details that do not drive the mission of the school forward such as "they let us wear jeans on Fridays." That answer does not showcase your dedication to the profession or reflect what you need and want in a leader.

• *What is your behavior management style?*

Interviewers want to know how you set expectations, teach appropriate behaviors, and hold students accountable in a supportive and loving way. For example, you might want to avoid saying something like "Well, if they didn't follow the rules, they would lose a privilege." Although this sounds logical, the child will continue on the same path because you have not reinforced the correct behavior; instead, you have provided a consequence for the wrong one. You might want to say something like "If students do not follow a classroom rule, I will remind them of the rule, ask how their behavior differed from what the rule stated, and together set a goal for following the rule moving forward." This shows that you are proactively helping the children achieve behavioral success in the classroom by assuming they did not know how to follow the rule, reminding them how, providing them time to reflect (consequence), and then washing the slate clean and moving forward.

• *How do you incorporate parents into your classroom?*

This answer depends strictly on the clientele of the school. Schools range anywhere from low to high parental involvement, and many factors contribute to this. Share your philosophy on parents being involved in their child's education. Since you did your homework when researching the school, you will have specific information to personalize your philosophy during your interview. This tells the principal that you know about this school and already have a plan to tackle parent involvement. For example, you might say, "My personal philosophy is that parents are essential in a child's education. We need to work together to help a child grow and succeed both inside and outside the classroom. However, I know at this school many parents are not able to volunteer and get as involved as I would hope. But I understand it's not a lack of interest to participate on their part. Many of these parents work two jobs and are the only parent in the home. My job when I begin to teach here is to create a relationship with the parents and let them know that I want them to get as involved as they can be. It might mean that I send home a project I need help creating, and in their free time they help cut out materials and send them back to school when they are finished. Just because they cannot physically volunteer during the hours of eight to three does not mean they can't help, does not mean they don't care, and certainly does not mean they are uninterested. My goal is to have parents get involved in the time that they do have for the benefit of each student."

• *How do you use data to inform your instruction?*

This is a difficult question when you haven't really had your own class yet. Hopefully you had a cooperating teacher who taught you how they collected data. If not, stating something like this should suffice: "Data is important because it helps me see what students know and don't know. But it also shows where there is a gray area that we need to revisit and firm up. Sometimes additional practice cures that on its own, but sometimes I need to just rephrase something, and it corrects itself. Overall, I am constantly watching my students perform through discussion, homework, and classroom assignments to make my instructional decisions. At the end of each day, I write down any 'ahas' to alter my instruction for the next day. I also use a check sheet for certain aspects of a topic I want to see students master. For example, 'Use the word *congruent* when describing shapes.' I'll consult my check sheet to see who got it, who didn't, and who explained the concept without using the word. This helps me pull small groups before diving into the next day's lesson."

• *What is your plan for preparing students for the end-of-the-year assessment?*

The interviewer wants to hear about your skilled approach to teaching state standards in a fun, engaging way but also hear that your students master the objectives throughout the year, so you do not have a "test blitz" at the end of the year before the test. Many schools purchase test prep materials, but you'll want to shine here by explaining how you are so in tune with your students' academic achievements that you will not wait until the end of the year to begin a review. Rather, you will spiral skills (reteach concepts already introduced) throughout the year so your students' knowledge strengthens and grows through multiple opportunities. You, of course, have a backup plan for students who have not quite mastered those skills, but it won't be many students because your individualized instructional approach caught things early and helped build the foundation. This way, all students are successful.

• *How do you ensure students with special needs are receiving their accommodations and meeting state requirements?*

This is especially tough when you may not have had students with an IEP (Individualized Education Plan) or PEP (Personalized Education Plan) in your student teaching. However, at this point you can share your philosophy and plan of action with the interviewer. You might say something like "I believe all students can achieve at high levels when they are supported in the classroom the way they need to be. So, when I receive the paperwork stating what a particular student needs in the classroom, I will review the document thoroughly and include on my lesson plans where to provide those accommodations. If I notice the accommodations are limiting or not supportive enough, I will reach out to the special education team for help in providing the best educational environment for that child."

- Prepare a few questions of your own. Your questions should showcase the research you conducted in the previous step, because taking time to investigate details shows your interest level in the job. For example, you might say, "I noticed your test scores were strong in reading. Is there something you require of your teachers to ensure that growth occurs each year?"

Exude confidence. Once you have been granted an interview, all of your preparation up until this point is your foundation for a successful meet-and-greet. It's showtime! Follow the tips below to have a successful interview:
- Show up early and introduce yourself to the secretary. While you wait, run through your interviewing scenarios to calm your nerves.
- Bring a few copies of your résumé for the interviewers and a piece of paper and a pen to write down information gained during this meeting. It is always a good practice to bring a backup of everything in case something runs out or breaks.
- Dress professionally, not stylishly. At this point, your personality will show through with what you have to say, not what you wear. You don't want to distract the interviewer or be remembered for what you wore, because what you say and do is more important than clothing.
- Bring a bottle of water to remain hydrated while you speak at length. Use caution, as too much water will make you have to end your interview early to rush to the restroom.

- Smile. Smile. Smile. Pretend you already have the job and are just meeting the principal to discuss logistics of your job. That does not mean you should walk in cocky; rather, be personable and relaxed.
- If you need time to think of your answer to the interviewer's question, you can repeat the question in your answer while you think, ask for a moment to collect your thoughts, or jot ideas on paper as the question is being asked.
- Practice a firm handshake and maintain eye contact, even during awkward pauses. This demonstrates your confidence in yourself to be part of their team and to do a great job for their students every day.

Have patience. Relax, the hard part is over. You survived the interview process and lived to tell about it! Below are some tips to follow after you have interviewed at a school:
- Write down any questions the interviewer asked you that you were not prepared for so that you can have a well-developed response for the next interview.
- Do not overthink every response you provided during the interview. There is nothing you can do about it now. Just focus on the road in front of you. You can be thankful for the opportunity and grateful you were as prepared as you were.
- Follow-up with a thank you note. You can e-mail or send a personal note of thanks to the principal for taking time out of his or her busy schedule to meet with you. Include a personal tidbit from your time spent together so the principal knows it was not just a "copy and

pasted" form letter to multiple interview sites. This again shows your level of interest in a school.

- ○ A quick note: School districts have hiring policies that vary, so you may not hear a response at all. In my school district, the principal calls Human Resources (HR) to recommend you for the job, and then HR calls you to offer you the position. I have seen it take an hour or up to a month, depending on the time of year and level of need. It is appropriate to reach out to the principal you met with after a week if you have not heard anything. At that point, he or she may tell you: a) the position has been filled, or b) a decision has not yet been made and someone will contact you shortly. Do not hound the school staff, students or parents.

- Continue interviewing because putting all of your eggs in one basket is not a motto I would recommend. Besides, the experience can only help you become more effective in demonstrating your passion, talent, and intent. Spend time reviewing your résumé and brainstorming ways to beef it up with experience or skills for your desired job. Remember, the résumé is a working document, not engraved in stone. If you did not get your dream job, you have years ahead of you to still achieve that dream. Michael Jordan did not make the varsity squad of his high school basketball team because he was too short. Did he curl up into a ball and stop living his life? No, he worked harder so that when he was taller, he was prepared to play at the varsity level.

Dream big and then chase that dream into reality. I know you can do it!

Celebrate. You do not have to wait for a job offer to celebrate. After every call or e-mail you receive about your interview, you should celebrate those milestones regardless of the outcome because you are miles from where you started. Enjoy the journey and all of your hard-earned progress!

3
Being Professional

If you want to not only get a job but maintain a job, you need to remain professional at all times. Professional behavior can look and sound like many different things. To me, to be professional means you put your best foot forward in all situations, from the clothing you wear to how articulate your speech is. Being professional does not mean losing your personality or individuality. It just means you think before you act and present your best self in all situations. In the beginning, it might seem as though you are living two different lives. But I assure you, as you become wiser in years, your two lives will mesh, and you'll find yourself having to think less before you speak or act. A mature mind-set and life marry well with professionalism. Just keep reminding yourself, "I like my job. I want my job. I *need* my job." Therefore, you cannot do X, Y, or Z right now. The fruits of this labor will come, trust me! Follow the tips below to better understand the realm of professionalism:

Be a professional at work. The obvious first place to be a professional is at work. You must look the part so you can act the part. You do not need to break the bank to look professional. Teachers need to be comfortable, yet presentable. Do not take comfortableness as a green light to wear sweatpants and sneakers to work. Buy yourself a good pair of dressy slacks. You do not have to wear them every day, but you will need them in your closet.
Since the job requires teachers to be on the move constantly, the clothes and footwear need to rise to

the challenge. There are a few tests you can conduct prior to a purchase to ensure the item you are interested in can withstand a day in the classroom:

- If you raise your hands above your head and your shirt comes up to expose your stomach, do not buy the shirt.
- If you sit down on the ground with your legs crossed and your undergarments show, do not buy the pants.
- If you cannot walk around the entire store without your feet hurting, do not buy the shoes. When you buy a new pair of shoes, I suggest breaking them in first. Do not wear them to work the next day. Wear them around the house or your feet will look like a war zone covered in Band-Aids. Go through your closet and separate the dressy shoes from the weekend shoes. If they are missing material, stained, not polished, or otherwise in need of repair, do not wear them to school.

Now that we've covered clothing, let's talk about professional behavior at work.

- There are many events that your school will host each year. No matter what the event, make sure you show up on time, your room is neat and tidy, and you are prepared to mingle with parents. This is not the time to start cutting out your laminated items, search the internet for cute projects, or talk on a cell phone. All of that must be done before the parents arrive. Not only are you are representing the school, but you want to send a positive message that you value the parents' time and you are committing your evening to them wholeheartedly. During these parental interactions, remain positive and encourage a two-way dialogue. Ask parents questions to get to know them and their child better. No parent wants to come and be talked at for two hours. Say what is necessary to the whole group, and then allow parents to talk among themselves, ask you questions, and look around the room. When talking with parents, employ your professional language, which displays manners and a well-educated vocabulary. Avoid speaking too loosely or using slang so as not to be misunderstood.

- You will be planning quite often as a team in your grade level. This is not the time to start throwing accusations around and making snide remarks about a colleague you do not care for. Leave your differences at the door. Remain focused on the topic at hand. You do not have to like everyone, but you do have to respect them and act professionally.

- The staff lounge is a great place to watch how social hour can become a "cool clique" or a "bashing brigade" for students, teachers or parents. Many teachers choose to eat lunch in their own classrooms to not only get work done but also to avoid the drama. I have always loved eating in the teacher's lounge because it is quiet, and I can have an adult conversation. Besides, I had been in my classroom all morning and needed a change of scenery. But, because I made the decision to eat in the staff lounge, I also made the choice to talk about school in a positive light (leaving all moaning and complaining to be done at home), or talk about life outside of school. It was hard in the beginning, but each day the choice became easier, and I quite enjoyed my time there.

Be professional in public. Being a professional when you are off the clock can be tricky. You represent the school district and school you work for, and what you say and do reflects that place of employment. You are allowed to be human, dress comfortably, and act yourself. But I caution you to be thoughtful about where you go and when you go there.

- I did all of my shopping near my home and not near school, so I could avoid impromptu parent-teacher conferences, avoid students seeing me in less-than-my-best garb, and enjoy an overall sense of relaxation during my shopping experience. Some of you will not have that luxury and will be faced with students and parents at all times. Therefore, before leaving the house, check your outfit in the mirror. A tank top might need to be covered, short shorts might want to be replaced, makeup might require a light touch-up! Also, read what your T-shirt says. If it displays an inappropriate logo or product, cover it or change your shirt. Your school's reputation is based on your actions. Make a good impression.
- If you wish to celebrate your Friday at an establishment where you must be of age, do not wear school paraphernalia. (Guilty as charged on numerous occasions.) Not only are you being judged on what you wear but how you act. Be careful with what language you use because you never know who is listening.

Be professional online. Much of my communication with parents was done online through e-mail or text apps on my phone.

- Write out your e-mail without including e-mail addresses so you can proof it for spelling and grammar errors first without it accidentally being sent out.
- Include parent e-mail addresses in the blind carbon copy [BCC] section so all those receiving the e- mail do not have access to each other's e-mail addresses without proper consent.
- Ensure you are creating a two-way dialogue, so you are not just talking *at* parents. Yes, most of your e-mails will be informational and need to be teacher directed. But do not forget to have a personal conversation with parents about their child every now and again. There are lots of great things going on at school with your students, so share information about them! Parents know their children the best and can often give you some helpful hints.

If you are networking with other educators, do so in a positive and professional manner. Many social networks can get negative quickly and before long the author of the post is in trouble. What you say on the internet can be held against you. Do not speak specifically about a parent, student, staff member, school, or district online. In fact, just keep anything negative to yourself. Teachers have lost their jobs over what was posted online (photo or written comment), so think wisely before interacting online. If you want to highlight your school in a positive way, that is also your choice. However, speaking in general terms might help avoid potential pitfalls and misunderstandings.

4
Getting Settled

Now that you have your first teaching job (Congratulations!), you are ready to get the preparation for teaching underway. Getting settled refers not only to organizing supplies and a workstation, but also to readying your mind. You cannot jump into a job effectively if your head is not in the game. Your nervousness should have subsided by now because the hard part is over...well, for now! Thorough preparation will ensure a smooth transition for not only yourself and your students, but also your colleagues.

Teaching is rewarding, but difficult. Prepare as much as you can so you can handle its obstacles. If you think it is going to be a cakewalk, don't go any further. Turn right around and do something else. If you are up for the challenge, buckle your seat belt and continue reading.

Due to my Type A nature, I like organized lists and reference points, so I have neatly categorized my ideas for the most effective mental and physical preparation. Let's focus on how you can do your job well!

Attend all beginning of the year [BOY] meetings. There are so many details to work through at the beginning of the year, and if you are new, there are a lot of staff names to remember. Bring a notebook to meetings and record everything. You might find it helpful to make a chart that includes people's names and titles, so you know who to go to for what (example: John Smith - computer teacher). These meetings might make your head spin in the moment, but you'll be glad you stored all of the important information in one place, like a notebook, when you digest it in pieces in the comfort of your couch that night.

Calendar the year out. Take the calendar you receive at the beginning of the year (or online if your district supplies it) and place all workdays, holidays, and special events on it. Get a desk-sized calendar for school and place the same dates there. This way you are organized and can adequately plan around those specific events throughout the year. Know that all calendars are not final, so use pencil!

Check out the furniture setup. Spend time in your room walking around to get a feel for the space. Where can you see yourself being the most comfortable? You will most likely stand in that spot often, so make sure all of the students can see you and all materials are accessible from that point. Before you move student desks, draw the configurations out on paper first. Not only is the process loud, but your back will thank you later for planning ahead. And don't forget to check for electrical outlets that specific furniture will need to be close to, like computer tables or reading lamps!

Create detailed name tags. Most schools require students to wear name tags on their bodies at all times when they are in the school building for safety and identification purposes. Whether the name tags are computer or teacher generated, it is a good idea to include important information such as the student's first and last name, ID number, transportation method, lunch number, library checkout number etc. Feel free to add other important information as you see fit.

Design a class schedule. Some schools allow you to create your own daily schedule. In those cases, it can be best to place the subjects with the highest cognitive load in the morning when students are bright-eyed and fresh-faced. Placing subjects with movement or excitement after lunch or recess is also recommended. If you work at a school where you cannot design your own daily schedule, most likely because of sharing staff for instructional support of particular students, be sure to follow it as closely as possible. For example, a teacher assistant might be assigned to your grade level for a short period of time each day to support English language learners in Social Studies or Science. Getting off-schedule can be a detriment to those students who require additional assistance.

Establish rapport with the principal. Start a conversation with your administration that is not related to school. You want to ensure that you get to know them on a personal level. There will come a time when your positive relationship with them will come in handy—most often when you are stressed and lack confidence in your ability to wake up another day to teach. Take control by creating the impression of yourself that you want them to have. Don't allow a future unforeseen situation create their impression of you.

Get a buddy. You will have a bad day. Find someone who is in the same boat to cry, laugh, and vent with you. You will need to relieve stress and rejuvenate, or you will lose your mind. As mentioned in a previous chapter, though, you will need to take caution in whom you decide to confide in so that it remains a safe place to vent. Choose wisely.

Get a flash drive with *loads* of room. Set up desktop folders by quarter, then by subject, and then by assignment. This way, when you go to locate a specific file, you'll know exactly where to find it instead of perusing an endless number of files. You will use files year after year so having an organizational system to locate files quickly is very helpful. (I used to save reading comprehension files by the title of the passage instead of what it was used for and I could never find it! For example, "Sam's Flowers" versus "Quarter 3 Reading Formative.")

Keep a diary. A reflection journal is helpful to get out nervous or anxious feelings. You will need an outlet for all the emotions you will be feeling, and you don't want to bring that with you to school.

Know the buzz. Just like the acronym overload, there are some educational buzz words you will hear so often you might just get sick of them. But you will continue to hear them until you can do them. And you cannot do them if you do not know what they mean. During staff meetings and other professional development opportunities, these buzzwords will appear and most often are considered non-negotiable instructional approaches with the principal. I kept this list short, knowing that by the time this book gets published a million more words will surface, and school districts value different approaches to teaching and learning. As mentioned before, if it is brought up, *do it*. Give it a shot. No one is asking you to be an expert; they just ask that you try. Reach out for help and ask questions. Being transparent is a quality many people wish they had but are too prideful to become. Make that your strength and shine as the newbie risk-taker! Here are the words I hear most these days:

- Active engagement
- Differentiation
- Inquiry-based learning
- Meaningful feedback
- Project-based learning
- Relevancy
- Rigor
- Student-centered instruction
- Technology integration

Make a seating chart. A seating chart is not only helpful when planning which student sits where, but it is also a great reference to keep in your lesson plan or grade book as you design lessons in terms of student groupings and movement. It is a great tool for anyone taking over your class, too (i.e., assistant and substitute teachers). I, however, recommend that you make it more specific than just a floor plan with a student name on a desk by adding student learning characteristics under their names.

- Create a Word document and configure a table that works best for you (I used four rows and five columns).
- In the table, place each student's name and behavior/learning trigger words to help you in planning lessons and rearranging student learning groups. These characteristics (e.g., talkative, needs visuals, or requires manipulatives) will change as students learn, grow, and adhere to classroom protocol. This is especially useful for other teachers who help in your classroom without you having to debrief them on your students if you need to step out for a minute.

Meet parents and students at Open House/Meet the Teacher Night. When you are meeting your incoming class for the first time, you will want to connect with them on a personal level but be careful not to get too casual. You want to showcase your personality and make your room inviting but you also want to establish authority. So, wait until school actually starts to show off your dance moves to the latest song with them. They will like you more if they respect you first. First impressions matter. Be personable and warm, shake hands, and make eye contact. Don't forget to repeat those names! You will be saying them often in the upcoming year.

Meet staff and students. Anytime you meet someone be sure to make eye contact, shake their hand, and smile! If you are introduced to a colleague, ask them their last name as you will rarely call them by their first name, especially in front of students. So, you might as well not waste your brain cells committing a name to memory that you will never use. Once you are told a staff or student's name, refer to them by name as often as possible to help you recall it later. If you cannot remember names, do not be hesitant to ask. It's better to ask now while you have the "new person" label still attached to your forehead, rather than getting embarrassed months down the line not knowing their name.

The mistake many teachers make is only getting to know those individuals they consider the "most important" people in the building, which to them is often the administrative staff. This misconception will lead to a year full of frustration. You must get to know the right people — the people you will call on to help you anytime you need something, such as the cafeteria staff, custodial staff, and the secretary.

The cafeteria staff hook you up with delicious "extras" and let you get away without paying a time or two. (When I was selling jewelry as a side job, my cafeteria staff were my number one customers...so don't underestimate that relationship!)

The custodial staff is your saving grace. You will forget your keys to your classroom often and get locked out. They will unlock your door for you before you get to school in the morning so when your hands are full, you don't have to put things down. You will need a mess cleaned up in your classroom that you created and want no one to know about. They will clean your room with extra care because you make them feel important. (My custodian worked at my previous school with me too, so we were tight. He was my right-hand man. Each day he cleaned my room first after school so we could chat before I headed out to my next job. Don't underestimate that relationship!)

The secretary knows *everything* about what is going on in the school. I used to ask my principal questions relating to particular students until I realized the secretary knew each parent, each child, and all the drama in between. The secretary is easy to find and a wealth of knowledge. (The secretary at my previous school would call me privately to remind me to input attendance if I forgot instead of paging me on the intercom for all to know. She selected just the right student to be my next "new" student because she knew that child's situation was perfect for my teaching approach. She looked out for me. Again, don't underestimate that relationship!)

Sometimes, the best people to get to know are the ones considered at the bottom of the food chain.

They're humble, reliable, and work hard. They are the strength behind the impact we had as a school because without them, all the "behind-the-scenes" duties would take us away from what we should be focusing on: student learning. I thank them for their positive attitude and mind-set.

Memorize terms. There is a laundry list of terms and acronyms that teachers sneak into every conversation at school. You will have a hard time making sense of educational conversation without the understanding of what the terms stand for. As mentioned before, never be afraid to ask. Here are some of the terms I used often in conversations with colleagues:
- RTI (Response to Intervention)
- API (Academic Performance Index)
- AYP (Annual Yearly Progress)
- ELD (English Language Development)
- ELL (English Language Learner)
- ESL (English as a Second Language)
- FAC (Faculty Advisory Committee)
- TAC (Teacher Advisory Committee)
- ILT (Instructional Leadership Team)
- 504 (accommodations under Section 504)
- IEP (Individualized Education Plan)
- PDP (Professional Development Plan)
- LRE (Least Restrictive Environment)

Organize copies. If you have an amazing team of coworkers, you will plan together and even make copies for one another. Make sure to prepare for the paper trap! You will receive copies for the day's lesson and subsequent lessons, so have a folder designated by day for each of the copies. Organization will save you time and allow you to focus on student learning. Besides, you'd just have to add "find those darn papers" to your to-do list, and no one wants to *add* anything to their to-do list.

Overcome the statistic. Teaching is hard. It is overwhelming and requires a lot of patience, reflection, and drive. Students, parents, and staff can get the best of you if you let them. The statistics prove that many teachers do not hang around long enough to really get the hang of their craft. Do not walk out the door because you feel overwhelmed, ineffective, or unsupported. It is normal to feel those things in the beginning. If you try suggestions given to you, reach out for help, and maintain a positive attitude, you can make it through. Do you want to get off the ride when it's in the air? Or wait until after you have the perspective of going from beginning to the end and appreciate the dips and turns along the way? Have faith. It will come together in the end. The kids deserve you, and you deserve them. Hang around.

Over-plan expectations. Plan exactly what you want your students to do, from where they stand to how they stand to what they stand with. If you cannot imagine what it should look like, you won't be able to clearly explain it to them, and they won't rise to the expectation. Spell it out. Spending time up front will save time later.

Over-plan lessons. Be sure to include additional information and tasks in your lessons in case your students understand the warm-up and maybe even most of the lesson faster than you planned; these students are referred to as "early finishers." You can easily divert to this plan without having to think on the spot (which can be another inefficient use of time). You'll need prepped materials for this too. You might think that planning a lesson is hard enough, let alone accounting for faster and slower learners. But it is not wasted time because you'll use it now or later. Plus, you're increasing your skill tool belt!

Plan for the short and long term. It is great to plan for the following day or even that same week. But you need to actually plan in advance to have clarity on how your lessons build on each other in the long-term and will meet all required objectives set out by the state and/or district. This method is called "backwards design." It is important to know how long you have to teach a particular topic (calendar and pacing guide) and how in-depth you need to teach it (objective).

- **Unit or quarter:** Map out future lesson topics on a blank calendar for each quarter. Mark off holidays and workdays so you know how many actual days you will be teaching in that quarter. (Caution: Remember being flexible? This is only a plan and will change a lot due to class pictures, field trips, performances, fire drills, etc.)
    - **Tip:** Ask your principal for an entire day to plan for the next quarter with your colleagues. A substitute teacher can take over your class. This time allows you to get a big-picture sense of where your instruction is going and where students need to be skill-wise by a particular time frame. You will struggle if you try to just walk in one morning and start planning your day or week. You need time to think through it as a big chunk of time. Planning makes you a successful teacher, so prioritize it. Or you'll pay for it later.

- **Daily lesson:** Begin with the objective needed to be taught, choose the appropriate assessment to prove students understand and can demonstrate mastery of that objective, and then fill in the holes with the actual activity last.

Reach out to students and families in the summer. It is a good idea to draft a welcome letter to students and parents. This is a great way to introduce yourself and explain the year that lies ahead. Include a schedule if available, behavior system, as well as a quick autobiographical and philosophical statement. Don't be afraid to appear human by including your personal interests or stories because that helps parents and students feel connected to you before the year even begins. Remain positive throughout the entire letter to get your students excited to meet you and take on the year.

Save bulletin board paper. At the end of the year, you might need to cover something on your walls as you prepare for testing or to protect items during summer cleaning, and it works great. Repurposing is a teacher's best talent. This is not only economical and eco-friendly but is also a time-saver!

Sit in students' seats. One aspect of planning effective lessons is thinking through where students are seated for learning. You can start by planning student seating arrangements on paper. This helps ensure all student desks can fit in a particular arrangement in the room, plus you can think through who is sitting near whom to encourage positive and productive working relationships. You want all students to see the board and your instruction clearly, so once you have planned student seating on paper, sit in their actual seats to ensure they can clearly see and have access to the board or learning materials from their desk location. The best way to properly plan student seating arrangements, without wasting instructional time, is to sit in each student's desk prior to their arrival.

Sleep. The first day of school will wipe you out, as well as the first couple days. Until your body is used to waking up early, standing on your feet all day, and grading papers into the wee hours of the night, you will need excessive sleep. Pretend you are a teenager on weekends and sleep in until the day is half over. Your body will thank you! In order to be completely operable, I suggest getting eight hours of quality sleep. You will need to force yourself to go to bed early so you can wake up early. Forget the snooze button; the kids need you. You need time to relax, decompress, rejuvenate, and prepare for the day. So, get into school early before other distractions arise and get things done. Count on having trouble with technology and dedicate part of your morning to ensuring everything functions. If you go to play an awesome video clip showcasing plate tectonics only to find out the link is blocked, or your internet is disconnected, you waste time, and it makes your attempt at bringing learning to life a time-suck.

Stash your essentials in a nearby drawer. As I mentioned, your day is very crazy. You will need things and not be able to get your hands on them due to your schedule and unending to-do list. So keep items like chocolate, aspirin, deodorant, lip balm, and other necessities nearby.

Subscribe to an educational magazine. You'll want to keep up-to-date on what is current in education. Some evaluations encourage teachers to be knowledgeable of current events in education and will count your subscription and shared knowledge as going above the minimum requirements.

Wait on the permanent marker. Allow students to add to or drop from your classroom roster for the first couple of days before you go putting their cutesy name on everything.

Write ideas you want to try on index cards. Collect ideas and place them on index cards in a recipe box. You can add to this stash as often as you wish throughout the year. During breaks from school, you can revisit these ideas to mix it up and try new things when you return. Feel free to write on the card as you try things and make notes on how it went or how to make it better next time. This compilation will become your teaching secrets that you can pass on to colleagues, especially mentees or student teachers. What a great way to pay it forward!

Write everything down in one place. The life of a schoolteacher is utter chaos. A million things are happening and only one minute has passed. The first couple days you will be e-x-h-a-u-s-t-e-d. You might wonder why you do what do you, but I promise, your body will become familiar with the craziness and even secretly miss it when you let out for summer. Staff members are inevitably in and out of your room needing things from you, most often when you are in the thick of a lesson. Learn quickly that although you say, "Sure, I can get that to you by the end of the day!" as soon as the door closes behind them, your mind has already forgotten. As soon as I think I might have to do something, I write it down on a sticky note. I secretly love to cross things off my list (that Type A thing again!), but it does help to get everything done in the time frame you need to get it done in. The quicker you find a reminder system that works for you, the better. This will help you avoid missing deadlines that result in more work and stress to catch up.

5
Diving into the Nitty Gritty

You have prepared yourself physically and mentally. Now it's time to get to work! And by work, I do not mean a forty-hour workweek. I mean a forty-plus-hour workweek. Due to this busy schedule, you must learn to balance and prioritize your personal and professional life. Is there something that can be put off until tomorrow? If it is not a deadline, it can wait. Otherwise you will stay in your classroom until the custodians kick you out in the evening and show up again as soon as the building opens. This is admirable, but not healthy. Yes, there will be days when you have to stay to get it all done. But, on average, you must learn to manage your time so you can be productive and sane.

This chapter is dedicated to all the details you will need to think about in addition to teaching your detailed lesson plans. I refer to it as a juggling act, like a circus clown trying to successfully keep multiple balls in the air at once. The tips I have included in this chapter are things I learned over time (mostly through embarrassing "Oh, I didn't know!" moments). Now you can avoid those awkward experiences and look like a pro!

Like any organized teacher, I have alphabetized my thoughts:

Address behavior with the specific student who is misbehaving. Creating change requires trust and trust cannot be established if students are embarrassed in front of others or if others are held accountable for someone's actions. Do not punish the whole class in a general statement. When addressing the misbehavior, be sure to explain why it is not acceptable and what the child should have done instead. This way they know how to follow the class or school rule going forward. In addition to not involving the entire class in redirecting a misbehavior, do not punish the whole class for problems with only one or a few students. There is nothing worse than being berated for something you were not involved in. Students do not need to know the mistakes or choices of others, so keep those conversations private and purposeful.

Alert the principal about an angry parent. Don't surprise your principal with an angry parent. Always give a heads-up when things are brewing. You're not a superhero, and if your principal is a good one, they will be there to support you first and foremost. As my father-in-law, a former high school principal, once stated, "An angry parent is a caring parent." Thank them for being involved and wanting the best for their child, and then propose solutions you both can agree on to best help the child.

Apply a consequence, then start over fresh. Students need to know they are loved before they can open up and take risks in your classroom. In order to be loved, they have to know you only judge their behavior and not them as a person. Show them that when you forgive, you forget. Build up your students by holding them accountable, accept the apology, and immediately turn to a fresh, positive page.

Ask questions. The best way to learn is by seeing teaching live. Watch your coworkers teach a similar lesson but in a different way. If you cannot physically be in the room at the time it is being taught, videotaping is a great tool. You might suggest your instructional facilitators videotape teachers who are willing to showcase their lessons so that those videos can be kept on file for teachers to check out and watch. What a great way to borrow ideas and learn from one another! Make use of your principal's open-door policy if he or she has one, but be sure to bring a solution too! Don't be afraid to reach out to your grade level chair, teammates, or mentor as well. There are a lot of people in the building ready and willing to listen to you.

Attend all trainings and take diligent notes. During the first few years of teaching, the district will require you to attend most trainings to ensure you are up-to-date on curriculum and teaching techniques. As you become more seasoned, don't get "too cool" for professional development [PD]. This is a great place to network, learn new approaches to learning, and have fun with other people who enjoy doing exactly what you do. You get out of it what you put into it. You'll always walk away having learned something worthwhile—personally or professionally. Be careful not to have a drive-by mentality where you sit and get but never use it. A workshop junkie does not remain a passionate teacher, so be purposeful in your learning. Choose to attend a workshop on a subject that you are passionate about or need to gain more knowledge about, and then decide what questions you need answered. Go participate!

Avoid the paper trap. Be sure to have an easy-to-use filing system during the day that allows you not to clutter your desk and find the necessary documents when you have a moment to organize them (e.g., student notes or tardy slips). If you have an established location to place paperwork, it makes locating what you need easier and quicker later. Do not throw things in one pile on your desk and expect them to sort themselves out, or worse, wait until a Friday afternoon to clean it up. Put things in their place in the moment or the pile will become a time suck. Start simple with "Keep" and "Toss" folders, or a "Do Now" and "Hang Tight" folder. You will receive tons of papers throughout the day and even more e-mails. They all need your attention so prioritize them by using an organizational system that fits your needs and style to avoid the evil paper trap. Whatever system you create, just use it consistently and require your students to adhere it.

Be clear on an objective versus an activity. Writing proper objectives can be difficult for newer teachers. Explain what skills the students will be demonstrating by the end of the lesson instead of putting the focus on what task they will be completing. For example, "compare and contrast qualities that define community types" versus "write an essay on the three types of communities." "Compare and contrast" references a skill students will learn whereas writing an essay is an activity. Writing proper objectives takes practice. Seek guidance from mentor teachers when needed.

Be consistent. In order to be successful in anything you do, you must be consistent. You have probably heard the phrase that it is not practice that makes perfect, but perfect practice that makes perfect. What you ask of students, and what they give you, needs to be consistent each time. For example, if you say to turn in homework in the same place each day, do not change the location or allow students to only turn in homework when they want to. Choose what you want, envision what it looks like, give expectations, practice expectations, require students to rise to the occasion each time and then celebrate. This is a process, so do not expect perfection on day one. Sometimes you will need to revisit these expectations, especially after a long break from school. You are the leader in the classroom so make the decisions and stick to them.

Be flexible. Understand that education changes constantly and what you walk into the classroom thinking you will do and how you will do it might change. Someone throws up in the middle of your science experiment and you must make a mass exodus for forty-five minutes while the room is cleaned and sanitized. Or your students might not understand square roots, so instead of teaching the lesson of new content, you review prior knowledge at a deeper level. Things happen. It is always good to have a plan, but understand it is only a plan. You cannot predict how the day will go. Learn to appreciate a day full of surprises, and do not groan when the clock is ticking and the school secretary is giving a ten-minute announcement on the intercom. Embrace the chaos and expect change. Being flexible will keep you sane, so adjust those expectations.

Be prepared at recess. It is a good time for students to get out their energy and focus on something they might be great at outside the classroom walls. It also gives you a chance to bond with your students on a personal level. I highly suggest bringing a recess bag with you that contains a whistle, hand sanitizer, Band-Aids, a cell phone/walkie-talkie, and a notebook. If you need to write a note for a student to bring to the nurse, you'll have paper to write on. Sometimes students get a tiny cut but may not need to report to a nurse for that, so having some cute Band-Aids saves time, and of course students love to sport the cool Band-Aid. Having a walkie-talkie or cell phone allows staff to get messages to you when you are not in the classroom. In terms of safety, recess is a bear.

Stand in a position where you can see your students at all times; scan so you can see all that might be happening, especially if there are multiple areas to play in; look for any item that might not be safe that you can remove to avoid any injuries. You can also use morning meeting time to talk with students about appropriate recess behavior. This can avoid lots of arguments and accidents later on. It is also important to ask administration what their expectation of recess time looks like, so you can follow protocol. (e.g., can students walk to reflect on assignments they did not turn in? Can teachers chat with one another or must you be spread out? How many classes can be on the equipment at one time?)

Bring energy and enthusiasm. Your students will reflect your energy level and enthusiasm for a subject. Have fun because you don't get this first year back!

Build relationships with colleagues. Build relationships with colleagues because growth and achievement stem from quality relationships with people who care. Find a support group of like-minded people and use this group to empower yourself, and vice versa. Be careful not to turn it into a negative experience by constantly sharing everyone's frustrations each time you meet. Spend some time getting things off of your chest, and then spend the rest of the time problem-solving or enjoying one another's company. Connecting as people and not just as educators can be a powerful way to rejuvenate.

Be unpredictable in your questioning patterns. If students know that once you call on them you won't come back to them the rest of the period or day, they will tune out. Make sure students hang on to your words by knowing your expectation is full participation even if they are not called on. You might just call on the same student two times in a row to ensure they remain focused and present.

Be yourself. Don't try to be someone else. Spend time figuring out who you are as a teacher instead of parroting the many great teachers you have seen or look up to. Although there are undoubtedly great aspects about those teachers that you could weave into your own teaching, you still have to develop your own voice and style. In addition, your students will dictate your decisions, so do not compare yourself to other teachers who do not have your same students. What works in your classroom with your kids is different than what will work with others, so stand up for what you know is best for your particular students.

Break big projects into bite-sized "check-in" dates. At first, students can be poor managers of time, especially when they have a lengthy block of time to complete a task. As adults, we know how to plan backwards to complete all necessary tasks within a specific time frame. But many students have not perfected that skill yet. There are a few strategies you can implement to help students develop time management skills.
- First, teach them to use an agenda or calendar to write due dates down. Eventually they will be able to use that final date to work backward with mini due dates to ensure they remain on track to finish all requirements on time.

- In the meantime, you can model that practice by placing reminders of those mini due dates on the board, so students see them each day. This means you will assign portions of a larger project for homework to ensure students are completing bits and pieces of it as the days pass by.
- Last, provide a timeline or checklist to help students track their progress.

Call parents for behavior. When it comes to parent contact, be sure you have established a positive relationship prior to having to make a negative phone call or home visit. A pre-established relationship encourages parents to be open to hearing from you and trust that you have the best intentions when wanting to partner together for the benefit of their child.

Prior to contact, be sure you have followed school and class protocol for dealing with misbehaviors before getting to the point where you have to notify parents. (Many times, there is a standard sequence of steps to follow that increase in consequence.) In the cases where parents do have to be notified, students can immediately become detached from learning the rest of the day because they are either a) hoping to tell their parents first by formulating a plan of attack and storyline to avoid getting into trouble when they arrive home or b) knowing you have already contacted their parents, they are now fearing the trouble they will be in when they get home.

To avoid these two scenarios, contact the parents together with the student. Allow the student to tell their parents their misbehavior or the class or school rule that wasn't being followed. They then should describe what they plan to do differently in the future. If you need to add details for clarity, you can do so at this point, but often when the child is sitting with their teacher talking with their parents they stick to the facts and no additional clarity is needed. Parents appreciate the "team" concept in communication as well as their child being the one to step up and admit their wrongs while also sharing their ideas for how to move forward. It is a life lesson in maturity and accountability.

Check for understanding [CFU]. Don't wait until the end of a lesson to see if students understand what you are teaching them. Check students' understanding of material after each portion of the lesson, meaning after the directed, guided, and independent practice sections. There is no reason to continue a lesson if students are not with you. You will further confuse them and not make good use of your time. Ensure the majority of your class comprehends the content before proceeding to the next section of the lesson and pull a small group to reteach concepts for those who do not fully understand.

Collaborate with colleagues. You do not need to plan lessons by yourself. Make use of the experienced staff around you to plan the best lesson possible. There is no reason to start from scratch; use the expertise of your colleagues to your advantage! You will never become better by working by yourself. Collaborating empowers all of the individuals involved. A shared planning time allows a team of teachers to talk through pacing guides, objectives taught, and how to best use student performance data. You might even want to talk with specific teachers in order to get a sense for how long something takes to teach and for ideas on how to teach it. This is a great time to get on the same page and have support from expert educators in areas you might need. Ask lots of questions and contribute your ideas, regardless of how much experience you have. They value you, or you wouldn't have been hired in the first place. Oftentimes, veteran teachers love to hear from newer teachers because you have fresh ideas that are cutting edge and super engaging to students, so share!

Control from the middle. It can be tricky to find the perfect place for you to stand when walking with students in the hallway. If you take the lead in the front of the line, you are able to guide students to their destination, but you miss all of the misbehaviors happening behind you. If you walk at the end of the line, you are able to catch all of those misbehaviors in action, but the front of my line can struggle with where to stop or turn, and even at what pace to walk. Try standing somewhere in the middle where your eyes can efficiently scan all students and keep them on task in the hallway while also guiding students to their next destination.

Create a "babble-free zone." When delivering a lesson, don't babble in front of the room. Instead, choose your words and make them purposeful. Otherwise, you will lose your audience and credibility. This is an example of "don't cry wolf." When you are concise in your wording, your students value and hang on to each word you say.

Drill the drills. During the first week of school, you will generally need to review procedures for fire, tornado, and lockdown drills. It's essential you not only explain the importance of the drills but model student actions during the drills. Your principal will probably ask you to run these drills with your class the first week and prepare for an unannounced practice as a school during the first month. Ask colleagues which drills you need to prepare students for. If students have attended the same school the year prior, they are already familiar with the procedures, but an emergency is not the time to refresh their memory. Practice each drill throughout the school year to ensure it becomes a habit, so when you are called to action, it happens naturally.

It would be helpful for you to prepare some items ahead of time as well. You may choose to create visuals of these procedures for students and post them up in the classroom as a reference when needed, especially when their nerves take over in a stressful situation.

Most importantly, you'll want to create a binder that includes a student roster so you can do a roll call and parent contact information to leave by the door and grab on your way out for all drills and/or emergencies. Don't forget your cell phone!

Embrace walk-throughs. The state and district require the administrative team to walk through classrooms on a continual basis to ensure the learning occurring in those classrooms adheres to the expectations (academics, behavior, etc.). Sometimes the administrative team is looking at a specific component of instruction for all teachers and other times they are just popping in to see how things are going. Whether you receive formal feedback or not from these visits, know it is a way to ensure great teaching and learning is happening for every student in the building and not a way to continually point out areas of improvement.

Engage all learners. One of your biggest tasks as a teacher, besides delivering content, is to be engaging while doing it. There are tons of ways to engage students — just ask your colleagues or do a quick internet search — but some strategies I suggest are to have students repeat instructions; have students respond to one another, not just the teacher; allow movement whenever possible; and allow stretching or brain breaks to split up a long sitting period. For some high-energy students, give them a job to do to get out their energy and be involved in the class, like being in charge of turning on/off lights for presentations or videos. It's a chance for those students to be successful with their energy rather than distracting.

Establish routines and expected behaviors. The first week of school is spent getting to know one another and the classroom. Part of getting to know the classroom is learning how to move about in it, also called "transitioning." Think ahead of time about ways students should move around the room. Smooth transitions that last seconds instead of minutes can be achieved through practice, the use of a timer, as well as having teacher and student materials laid out and ready to go. Practicing transitions in an efficient way allows quality learning to occur each and every minute.

You must have routines in the classroom for just about everything. You might think that trying to be in charge of the minutia in your classroom is just an effort to control your students' every move. But students thrive in a structured environment and routines create that structure. From the moment students enter the classroom until the time that they exit, there needs to be routines in place for their behavior and academic performance. Procedures will save you time in the long run, make your classroom run smoothly, and gain you days' worth of instructional time when you consistently enforce the procedures.

You might assume students know what you want them to do, and you might even assume you know what you want it to look like. However, even though you have thought through the ideal scenario, that doesn't mean student behavior will actually mirror the scenario. Students might behave in a way you have not thought of, or they might ask a question you didn't prepare an answer to, and you're stuck in the moment not sure what to say. Think through as many scenarios as possible ahead of time so you can create a plan of attack, teach it, and have students practice it. Plan procedures, teach procedures, practice procedures, and practice some more.

Create a list of routines and procedures that you want to teach and then prioritize that list from most to least important. Choose a handful of routines you will teach on day one. If you give your students too many routines to remember, they will not be successful. The next day, practice the previous day's routines and add a few more. Repeat this process until students are in a good flow. Remember, be consistent! Your routines should be the same each day rather than a routine for a very specific once a year activity. If you are going to have an expectation of students, you need to inform them before holding them to it. Allow students to practice these routines and procedures in the beginning until they get the hang of them. Then, praise and hold students accountable as they do them on their own. Eventually, they can perform these procedures without your help, but you might just decide to place visual reminders in those areas for student reference just in case. Example routines are:

- Attention-getting signal
- Enter/exiting the classroom
- Getting and returning learning materials
- Getting a tissue
- Greeting students at the door
- Morning work
- Sharpening pencils
- Throwing out trash
- Turning in assignments
- Using the restroom

In addition to the routines themselves, you will want to plan ahead for potential behavior pitfalls (e.g., Can everyone fit in a learning area? Are materials easily accessible for all students? Is there an efficient, orderly way to enter and exit? What is an acceptable volume for this routine?)

Execute wait time. One strategy to get more participation from students in a lesson is to pose a question and then wait. Your lessons do not need to move at the speed of light with little downtime. Although you want an efficient lesson with limited distractions, allowing time for students to process before responding is very powerful. Know when to be quiet and let students think. The first hand that goes into the air does not have to be the student you call on. Many students are capable of answering the question but could benefit from a few additional seconds. Talk slowly and provide time for students to process the information, formulate, and share a response. It may feel like a decade of waiting, but ten seconds ensures all students are thinking and learning versus just the most eager hand-raiser.

Expect dilemmas with a copy machine. The copier is a very hot commodity in a school building. It easily can get overheated or jammed with all of the activity. In knowing this, avoid making copies the day you need them. This means you need to plan what you need copied ahead of time to avoid potential hiccups like long lines, empty ink cartridges, and print jams. If you can, copy plenty of days in advance to avoid these issues. When it comes time to make your copies, ask around the school to figure out when the dead times are at the copier to ensure you maximize your planning time. If you do find the perfect unoccupied copier times, add a few minutes to your time frame to allow for the copier to turn on and/or heat up.

You can be even more efficient with your time if you make team copies of items. If your entire team of colleagues will be using the same worksheet for a lesson, dedicate one person to making the copies for the grade level and save the rest of you time. Just make sure you rotate this position so that it is a fair use of everyone's time.

Most importantly, it is always good to have a backup plan in case the copier is not available or broken for a lengthy period of time. If you are paper conscious, try only to copy things when it is absolutely necessary. For example, if your students can copy graphic organizers off the board rather quickly, providing a premade copy is not a good use of paper or time.

Find your "teacher" voice. You will often mirror your cooperating teacher, the lead teacher in the classroom where you did your student teaching, because it is the closest memory of teaching that you remember. But don't be afraid to create your own version of that model. You can even observe other teachers in your building to gather other ideas for how to lead a classroom. Ideally, you will want to be able to be firm and calm, yet approachable. In the end, be yourself, infuse your personality into your style, and have fun. You will be the most effective teacher when you are yourself.

Follow district pacing guides. Make sure you keep up with the expected pace and sequence of content that the district suggests. Most pacing guides are suggested calendars for what to teach, when to teach it, and how long to teach it — but it is flexible enough to adapt to your students' needs. Be careful to not teach concepts out of order unless you have district approval. Sometimes the district requires you to give a district-created assessment to your students quarterly, which means that the content on the test will be based on the pacing guide that they provided to you. It is okay if you are ahead or behind a few days due to being responsive to your students' needs, but you do not want to allow too much time to pass in the process. In all cases, keep your administrator informed if you are unable to keep up with the pace that the district suggests.

Get students working first. There might come a time where you need to take care of clerical work or speak with a student one-on-one. First, give students something to complete and then do what you need to do. You do not want students sitting idly as they will decide for themselves what to do to fill the time and that usually ends up in trouble!

Give directions, then let go. Require students to freeze during directions so they can hear them in entirety before following them. If not, students will immediately move or begin working and not hear the next step in the instructions. This creates a domino effect of unending "what do we do next?"- type questions. If students start moving while you are giving directions, stop them because what you have to say is important. Also, it is easiest if you number the steps in your directions and say them in the most concise way possible. This bite-sized, sequential method increases the likelihood that students will remember and perform the steps successfully.

Give specific feedback. If you want to build up your students' skill tool belts, you will need to provide specific feedback to their learning output. This will increase the likelihood for a favorable, correct response. For example, during a class discussion, you might say, "You are correct/incorrect because...." This helps students know your expectations so they can rephrase the material adequately. Be careful not to accept any vague answers. You might be tempted to add on to student responses to create a more thorough answer. Instead, prompt students with follow-up questions that will guide them to give you the full answer. This ensures they do the work and not you.

When it comes to written assignments, provide "glows" (areas of strength) and "grows" (areas of improvement) that are specific instead of just placing a stamp or sticker on their work. For example, you might say, "Johnny, you really hooked the reader by beginning your story with a question. Next time, try to use your five senses to add meaningful details that will help the reader visualize the plot." Now, the student knows what they did well and what to do better next time, thus improving their learning output. If you want to add a stamp or sticker in addition to the specific feedback, go for it!

Grade with a purpose. Grading papers can easily become your nemesis if you allow the pile to build up. Grade some papers daily so that the stack does not become overwhelming. In addition to that, you'll want to have a quick turn-around, so students can use your feedback in the next learning situation. You do not want them applying the same wrong logic to a similar situation when it could have been corrected sooner. Schools often require each teacher to have the same assignment count for report card grades, so check in with your team of colleagues to decide what assignments will be inputted into the grade book. That does not mean you stop assessing or providing practice assignments when you have reached your grade count. Instead, continue using student work as informal assessments to guide instruction. This has become a bigger issue in schools where parents feel their child has the advantage or disadvantage of being in a particular classroom based on what or how many assignments are given to students.

To avoid another big grade discrepancy, I also suggest you grade papers with a colleague until you get the hang of expectations and can be consistent with the team. However, do be prepared for your expectations of students to change as they grow. What you accept as "A" work in the beginning of the year is very different from "A" work you collect at the end of the year. I think it is important to discuss this with both students and parents. Explain your reasoning for allowing the change throughout the year and how it is beneficial to keep raising the bar.

Finally, some districts have put a failing grade policy into effect. For example, if a student receives a grade below failing, it is recorded as the highest failing grade (i.e. 60% equals an F so put 60 in the gradebook instead of the 32% that was actually earned). This is because it is too hard for a student to make a comeback after a zero or multiple low grades. To keep accurate records, use a paper grade book to record actual percentages earned, and then highlight it as a reminder that when entered into an online gradebook, it is changed to the highest failing grade. Be sure to check with your school district if this is the expectation.

Have a back-pocket activity. There will be times when your students sit idle as you rummage to find materials or set up an activity. When you're in front of your students and realize, "Oops! I forgot to...," have an activity they can complete while you do what needs to be done. This activity should be non-subject specific, so you can put it to use any time of the day. It should also be low maintenance, so you can give the instruction and students can begin within seconds. For example, you might have students turn and talk about a particular topic while you locate the copies you made earlier that morning.

Implement and track student interventions. There will be students who struggle in your class. The school will ask you to complete certain steps before they will intervene. Make folders for each student, ensure exact procedures are followed, and document everything to prove what you are seeing in class. For example, if a student does not comprehend material, provide documentation of specific instances where that was the case. Also, keep a record of how and how often you are helping the student in this particular area. This will help an intervention team plan a course of action.

Introduce a student question box. Some students are hesitant to participate in class for a variety of reasons. One way to encourage participation or ensure you provide clarity on any and all questions is to create a question box. Throughout the day students can write their questions on index cards and drop them into the box. Be sure to tell students that an appropriate question is one that is specific and academically focused. Then, at the next opportunity, you can read the question aloud and answer it in front of all students.

Lean on the experience of mentor teachers. If you have a mentor, this person was chosen based on experience and performance as a teacher. Don't be afraid to ask them anything! You can also reach out to the people whom you respect and look up to in your field. Talking to someone who is in the trenches with you helps convey perspective and actionable feedback. Ask detailed questions about how they teach a particular topic, so you can give it a try. "What worked for you when....," or "How did you handle...?" Or ask to observe them for a few moments in an area that is your weakness. Seeing teaching live is the best way to learn! These experienced teachers have learned on the job, and their stories will save you time by not falling into the same pitfalls, rather learning to walk around them!

Let grades inform instruction. If student test grades are pitiful, that reflects the lesson, not the student. Instead of penalizing students for an error on your part, let your grades inform your next steps as the instructor. You do not have to count that test if the majority of the class did not master the content. Simply reteach the lesson and revise the assessment so it is a fair and accurate depiction of student learning. Student performance mirrors your teaching. Give them the knowledge and time to work with it before they are asked to give it back to you. The point of a test is mastery of content. How can students test well if they are asked to recall information without the chance to retain it? (I'm especially thinking of your learning-disabled students.)

Let your students set the pace. You can be tempted to move quickly to finish your lesson plan on time or want to add in additional information because it could be interesting or sort of related to what you are discussing. But those two decisions can overwhelm and confuse students.

Don't over-teach by cramming too much information into one lesson as that is overwhelming for students. Wait until students have grappled with the subject matter and demonstrate a sufficient knowledge base before you add on to it. Overload creates a mind implosion, and the important things fall to the wayside.

In terms of trying to push through your lesson, recognize the learning needs of students who may need reteaching. This is the time when students desperately need the information slow and steady. If you rush to fit in a small group or try to finish all of your lesson plan points before time is up, you'll end up having to meet again with the small group to undo the confusion and anxiety you just created by rushing.

Having a time frame is important, but do not worry if you have to bump your mini lesson to another day to ensure students fully understand. In the end, student mastery is the goal, not following the ideal lesson plan or time frame.

Limit jokes and sarcasm. Joking around with students too often can send a confusing message. The more you joke around with students, the more relaxed everyone becomes, and that includes rules and procedures too. Before long, misbehaviors start to surface. Limit silliness, humor, and sarcasm during instruction.

Make bulletin boards reflect learning. Bulletin boards are a way to showcase student learning. Yes, they can be cute, but they most importantly should be interactive and reflective of instruction. Interactive means the audience passing by is encouraged to learn the material displayed by flipping pages in a foldable or answering a question that is posed. (Not all bulletin boards need to be interactive, but the ones that are tend to be remembered more often by students.) Reflective means it showcases the learning journey or destination students experienced in your class.

Make mental reminders. Remind yourself why you love your job, why you are good at your job, and why your kids are your tool for your own personal growth. There will be rough days but if you keep your mind focused on why you became a teacher, you will be able to remain positive and keep moving forward.

Manage behavior. Do not send students to the office each time they misbehave. Exhaust all of your options first so that you set the tone that you are in charge, you can handle it, and you will not tolerate misbehaviors. This shows your principal, your team, and your students that you are capable of being the leader in the classroom.

In the event that you have to send a student to the office, give administration a heads-up that a student is coming. You do not want the first time the principal is hearing about the student, incident, or behavior to be when they arrive on the doorstep of an administrator. Some teachers believe they are thought of as stronger or better by not utilizing the office as a form of consequence. This might be true in some instances, but if used sparingly and with good intention, it can be powerful in correcting misbehaviors. If you create a strong rapport with your administrative team, they know that when you send a child, it is a last resort and requires immediate attention.

If you are struggling to pinpoint the origin of student misbehaviors, consider how your actions and decisions are part of the problem or spark poor student behavior. Fix you first and then watch the domino effect take place (this might include confusing directions, disorganization, timid demeanor, etc.).

Manage the clock. There are a lot of things to take care of during the day so prioritize what needs to be taken care of first. There are not enough hours in the day, so your to-do list will often overflow into the next day or week. Check items off as you complete them and start a new list each week. If you do things in the order that they come, you will not be prepared in all situations. If you complete tasks based on their due date, you will always be on target. Sometimes due dates coincide, and you find yourself having a hard time completing everything to the best of your ability. In that moment, reach out to a mentor or administrator and share how you are committed to completing the task correctly but need a bit more time to do it.

Nip side conversations in the bud. If you overlook sidebar conversations, they will fester and become a larger issue. So, nip them in the bud. You can move closer to the students talking to encourage them to be quiet. Or lock eyes with them and pause in your speech. Let those students know that what you or any other person speaking has to say is important, so they need to listen.

Organize the day before. Just like you might lay out your clothes the night before so you're ready to go to work on time in the morning, try the same method at school. Before you leave the classroom, lay out your lesson materials and prepare anything necessary. Something will inevitably come up, such as your car runs out of gas, the school copier is broken, or you're locked out of your classroom, and you will not have enough time that day. Prepare *ahead of time* as much as possible. This will bring your anxiety levels down and help you operate efficiently. Don't put things off until tomorrow unless that due date is more than a day away because anything can happen!

Organize lesson materials. If you have filing cabinets, label each one with a subject/concept that you teach. Then place folders in the appropriate drawer for that content. Inside each folder, place all copies or materials for teaching that topic along with notes that you'll want to refer to before beginning that unit. These notes can be ideas for next time, things to avoid doing/saying, or ideas you heard from other teachers after the fact. This is something that takes time to build up and often won't be helpful until after you have a year under your belt to revisit the material you spent your first year compiling. Just remember: cabinet by content and folder by topic.

Outsmart e-mail overload. Carve out a time in your day to send and receive e-mails. In this day and age, e-mails arrive in our inbox constantly. It is tempting to read them immediately, but you need your full attention on your students at all times. Try to block out twenty minutes before and after school for e-mails. It is a common courtesy to respond to an e-mail within twenty-four hours, so waiting a few hours to check it is okay. Sometimes an e-mail is urgent, and you need the time you set aside to complete the task. Other times, you are able to get through all of your e-mails under the allotted time, allowing you to repurpose that time to complete other tasks on your list. Time management is a struggle for many teachers, so dedicating chunks of time to specific tasks is a great habit to develop.

Plan backwards. When planning a lesson, look at the standards and create the assessment first. Have you ever started at the end of a maze puzzle to find your way to the beginning? This is the same concept. Start with the assessment and then plan the lessons that lead up to that result, incorporating the skills needed to perform well on the assessment. Do not teach to the test! However, use the assessment to frame questions in a particular way, move student thinking to a higher level, and assure students have mastered particular skills on a topic. Then, take your own test so that you can find potential pitfalls easier and be proactive in adjusting the test, so it accurately measures students' knowledge.

Position yourself for authority and management. Stand so you can see all students in the classroom. Writing on the board with your back to the students only creates opportunities for misconduct. Stand in a place where you can view all students, so they know they are accountable in the classroom at all times.

Practice your lesson. A PowerPoint presentation is a great crutch for teachers. It is helpful in that it ensures you do not forget to mention all points in your lesson plan but standing in front of students and reading off a PowerPoint slide is not engaging. Don't PowerPoint them to death; interact with the material and students. Students need time to take in a visual, process the information, and react to it. It is not about you; it is about them. Deliver a teaching point, take a breath, and stay awhile. The more you internalize your lesson through practice, the more responsive you can be to your students' needs in the moment. You don't have to put on a dog and pony show. Sometimes something simple is more powerful than an exaggerated affair, but you need to be intentional about what you're saying and why you're saying it. If you happen to forget what comes next or need to reference your notes, don't let students see you sweat! Remain confident while you gather your thoughts. Your students do not know your lesson plan and will have little idea you skipped over something. Stay calm and your lesson will get right back on track without skipping a beat. (Calling attention to your flub will only encourage student misbehavior or increase potential for distrust.)

Provide clear directives for student participation. I highly suggest thinking about how you want students to participate during a lesson as this is often a gray area that gets exposed quickly and can allow chaos to ensue. Don't allow students to call out one moment and not the next because that sends conflicting messages. Stay consistent. If you want students to call out, ensure they call out. If you want students to raise hands, require them to raise hands. If you want to do a mix, be sure you are clear when the rules switch so they can meet expectations. For example, say, "Okay, we are going to do a quick review, no hands necessary."

Play music. I have become a fan of listening to free internet radio. I play it anytime I am in the room working. This helps me remain focused and calms any anxieties. I like that it drowns out excitement in the hallway, so I can stay on task and not get dragged into a juicy social conversation with colleagues. It is easy to be unproductive at school due to all of the distractions, so make sure you have a way to remain focused to get everything done on time. I also play music for students as they enter the classroom to create a calm, focused environment. When students are working silently at their desks, I play calm music in the background too. Music sets the tone and pace for learning.

Recycle lesson plans and ideas. Before planning a lesson, check with your colleagues for ideas and examples they have utilized in years past that you can replicate. This will save you time so you can focus on the execution rather than the creation of the content. When it comes to your own created materials, be sure to save your lessons and notes of all of your ideas to reuse the following school year. This ensures you do not recreate the wheel or waste time starting over year to year. It is also helpful to hold on to student work samples with the lesson materials, so you can show next year's class examples of finished products. Students are visual, and even with a rubric to guide the assignment, it can be more helpful to see an exemplar product. This will often build excitement and hook your learners.

Read up on your content area. One of the best ways to prepare to teach your content level is to read children's nonfiction books on any unfamiliar content you are teaching. In a children's book, the content is delivered in a simplified and easy-to-understand way. Then, you can scour the internet for more in-depth knowledge. Someone once told me that I don't have to know everything, I just need to know how to go about knowing everything. So start reading!

Reflect on student evaluations. Do you want feedback on how you are doing as a teacher? Ask your students! If you are feeling really brave, you can even encourage them to participate as honestly as possible by allowing anonymous feedback. This might encourage some students to say what they really want to say knowing they don't have to reveal their identity. Allow the honest feedback to make you better instead of taking it personally. There is always something that can be improved upon, and blunt feedback is the best way to gain another perspective on your instructional decisions. Plus, there's no better audience to give you feedback than the people who watch you teach all day. Their thoughts matter most.

If you are limited on their feedback, think through the following questions:

- How effective are you and your teaching strategies?
- How can you become better so that students can become better, instead of getting better just to get a bigger paycheck or a more prestigious position?
- Would you want to be a student in your classroom?

Scan the room constantly. Internalize your lesson plan as much as possible so you can be present and respond to students in the moment. It helps if you stand in a spot in the room that allows you to see most students and make eye contact as you do it. Students want to know that you notice them, especially when they are doing a great job. This also ensures you don't miss any minor misbehavior or signs of confusion so that you can act preventatively and responsively.

Shine during an observation. An observation, where an administrator comes to watch you teach and takes notes, is a time to shine. Thoroughly plan your lesson so it contains the necessary components and run through a practice of the lesson, so you focus less on the words coming out of your mouth and more on your students' response to the content. This is not the time to start something new the day of an observation. Be a risk-taker, but not on the day of an observation, especially if it is your first time trying it out. Go with tried-and-true methods to show off your skills. Then, the next day, take a risk and work out the kinks. The next round of observations will be there before you know it, and you can show off your risk-taking then.

Spend time with your students. Get to know your students as people and learners. You spend all day with them as learners. It is great to take off teacher and student hats and just enjoy being around one another as people. Be present and soak up the non-instructional seconds to bond with students. You will learn information about them that will help you design more effective lessons tailored to their interests and achievement levels. Some students shine when the weight of learning is taken off their shoulders. You do not want to let downtime turn into chaos, but do allow it to be bonding time between you and your students.

Start the day with a friendly, informative meeting. Having a time set aside for classroom community-building in your schedule is beneficial for any student at any age. You will increase the bond between you and your students, which fuels "buy in" for learning in the classroom. It is a time to set the pace and expectations for the day, such as announcements, celebrations, or reminders. There is always something to talk about, and students feel part of the cause when you involve them in a discussion.

Structure lessons. Misbehaviors can be avoided if you can structure your lesson appropriately. When you give clear instructions and have procedures in place, poor behavior is hard to come by. Be purposeful and proactive!

Think out loud. It is hard to teach students to think because you cannot access their thoughts as easily as they can. However, when you model your line of thinking, students begin to mimic this, and you increase their capability to problem-solve and draw conclusions.

Turn data collection into a simple process. Not everything has to be a formal test or run through a Scantron machine to show data. Sometimes your teacher instinct is spot on, but having a sticky note with a student answer to back up your feeling is the best type of informal data. There are classroom-friendly ways to collect data, like placing a student roster on a clipboard and jotting down quick notes while meeting one-on-one with students during the independent practice portion of a lesson. You might even want to reach out to mentors at your school to get a variety of ideas for how to collect and record data from your daily lessons. Create a data collection system that's easy to implement, fits your style and gives you reliable insight into student learning behaviors. It might be helpful to utilize one that can be applicable to various subjects, so you do not have to create a new system or tool for every assignment or subject.

Understand lesson plan design and requirements. Check with your administrative team to understand lesson plan expectations. Most schools have teachers plan through an online forum. The great news is the format is not as detailed as it was during your student teaching. Be sure to collaborate with your team. Creating great lesson plans does not make you a great teacher; it is what you do with them that is important. Lesson plans are constantly changing due to student needs, so don't feel like you need to follow your lesson plan to a T. You can make off-the-cuff decisions if it is in the best interest of the student. That is called "reflective and responsive practice."

Use every day analogies. Students love a good storyteller. If you can relate a difficult subject to a simple task like going to the movies, students can make connections and gain confidence to grapple with the new content. It takes the pressure off, entices students, and engages them in the task at hand. Being a relatable teacher makes building relationships with students easier.

Use a selective correcting method. There is not enough time in a day to correct every assignment that you give to students. You should make one of three decisions when it comes to grading: grade the entire assignment, grade a particular aspect (e.g., # 7 multi- step word problem because students have been struggling with that concept recently), or do not grade at all. If you decide to not grade an assignment at all, you can still collect it to ensure students completed it (maybe even assign a participation grade) or ask students to keep it. Sometimes you just want students to practice a skill without it being formally measured. This cuts down on the fear of failure. However, when you decide to correct an assignment, whether partially or entirely, let students do the actual correcting. This helps build ownership in the learning process. If you are able to provide a grading rubric for the assignment ahead of time, it increases the likelihood that students can meet the expectation.

Videotape yourself. This is a great reflection exercise when you don't have another set of eyes in the room. Videotape how you teach when no one is around. Watch your mannerisms, confidence, content delivery, and interaction with students. Move the camera to different areas of the room to see how effective you are from various viewpoints. This will help you correct behaviors such as teaching solely from one side of the room, calling on the same students, and using your hands or moving your body too much in a way that could be distracting. Administration is looking for larger indicators of success in a teacher's performance in areas like mini lessons, small-group instruction, and data utilization that they often do not give feedback on little things that a video will show, like body language. The best part is no one has to see the video but you!

Wear spirit attire. Many schools have a dress-down policy, generally on a Friday, where teachers can wear jeans and school colors. Not only is it very comfortable, but it brings unity to the school as everyone wears clothing showcasing their mascot or school colors. Students feel pride when they see all the teachers dressed just like them, supporting their school.

Write directly on your lesson plan. Don't be afraid to tweak your own lesson plan. After you taught something, take a second to write down what worked and what didn't, so that you can improve each time you teach that topic. Before you teach that topic again, you'll want to refer to how you taught it previously and apply the tweaks you brainstormed so that you can present the material more effectively.

6
Getting into the Groove

By this point, the newness of being a teacher has worn off, and you are settling in and getting into a groove. You might have begun this journey wondering if it would always be as hard as it is right now. Just like life is full of ups and downs, so is teaching. Starting any new endeavor is emotionally and physically exhausting until you start making the process work for you and get a handle on the workload. Teaching is not about instant gratification. Hang in there and do the work, and down the road you will be blown away to see how successful your students are because of your impact and influence. You are setting the foundation and expectations for students, and then setting them free. Your students are the future. There's no better job than this one!

The tips included in this chapter explain how to move beyond the basics in teaching. You are no longer brand new in the profession, have navigated the nitty-gritty details of the job, and are now in an autopilot groove. That's when you know it is time for an upgrade! Push yourself to continue your professional development journey so that you can better help your students reach new heights in their learning achievement.

Adapt your teaching style. Your principal will have a teaching style he or she prefers to see throughout the building. They strategically place teachers on teams to create the most effective group of teachers for a particular grade level. Oftentimes, very strong teachers with a unique approach to teaching will find themselves hitting their heads against the wall because their principal is not a fan of their natural instructional approach. But that doesn't mean you have to give up all of your unique ideas. You can mesh your personal style with the expectations of administration.

Principals love new teachers because of their energy and fresh content knowledge. Listen to what has been done before you and try what is being asked of you, before you begin testing the waters to define yourself as a teacher. There will be *plenty* of that to come.

Plus, giving the administrative staff what they want allows them to put their attention elsewhere, meaning they leave you alone for a bit. Ask your principal what "non-negotiables" they have during walk-through evaluations, so you can ensure you not only meet the expectation, but also exceed it. Nothing is a secret, especially if you are held accountable. Ask. Ask again. Ask some more.

Check your stress level. You cannot have energy to try new things in the classroom if you are stressed out. When you are new to teaching, everything required of you is overwhelming. Over time, you find your flow and manage the stress better. You will need to continue this same approach throughout your career as you are dealt new challenges and stressors. The biggest key is to sort through what is worthy of your stress... and it isn't the small stuff.

Co-Plan with special area teachers. One way to ensure students fully understand a concept is to revisit the concept multiple times in numerous ways. Let special area teachers (music, PE, art, computer, etc.) know the topics you will be covering in class in the coming months so that they can support you. By coinciding teaching concepts in multiple subject areas, you can enrich and deepen student learning.

Develop student independence. When students begin the year under your tutelage, they will be dependent on you and their parents to help them succeed. Your job is to take those training wheels off and help students learn to depend on themselves more as the year progresses.

This can be scary for parents and students so be sure to support both through it. It isn't going to happen overnight or without hiccups. There is something very powerful in failure. It builds drive, confidence, and perseverance. If parents are always doing things for their child, even providing reminders, the child never struggles, and those struggles can never develop the child's personal character.

Since it is hard to stop any habit cold turkey, parents and teachers can add responsibility at home and school little by little while decreasing support at the same time. It's uncomfortable for everyone because it is new and challenging. But it is the best thing for the child. As a teacher, you are only one human being helping twenty plus students learn and you cannot do everything for each of them all of the time. You do not want to be their crippling force, rather their elevating force!

Empower your students to share their strengths with others. What might drive you nuts about a student might be the single attribute that makes him or her successful in the future. For example, a chronic doodler could become a famous artist, a bossy student could become a leader of a Fortune 500 company, or a constant talker could become a world-renowned presenter. Get creative in how to use student strengths to the benefit of a lesson so that student's natural skillsets are sharpened.

Establish balance. Rest. Don't let yourself become "too" anything—tired, overwhelmed, or burdened. You have a lot of talent to share, so keep your priorities in balance in order to perform at your best. To be effective you must keep your spark. Take a deep breath and then take on the world!

Find your joy. Don't forget to celebrate your own progress, small or large. Keep a file for kudos from staff, students, or parents. Implement time at the end of the day, with or without students, to share the day's achievements. Discover what parts of your daily job that you enjoy and allow yourself to be fully present in those moments. Your joy will fuel your work.

Implement something new. Start your implementation small and add on something new each week once you have the hang of the previous item. Discuss your plan of attack with your mentor and principal. Then, prioritize how you will roll out these initiatives in terms of what has the biggest impact on student learning.

Integrate safe social media options into the classroom. Sometimes the best way to reach a difficult student is through his or her preferred communication tool, which is oftentimes social media. There are many tools out there that mimic popular social media sites and can become a great communication (or even assignment completion) tool to implement into the classroom. Teach students about internet safety and etiquette. By building their interests into instruction, you are letting them know that you value them.

Mix up your lesson format. Routine is important for student learning, but monotonous repetition can turn off learners quickly. You want to avoid desensitizing your students to your amazingly engaging lessons by repeating the same format or flow day after day. Try to mix it up to keep student interest alive. Be sure to always provide an activity to practice the newly learned knowledge, regardless of how you decide to mix up the delivery. If you keep a stringent routine, students tend to zone out. But, if you keep it fresh and interesting, you can keep their attention while also increasing student achievement and engagement.

Network with other teachers. Networking can be the best professional development opportunity teachers have at their disposal. It doesn't have to be limited to just your school or district. Don't let school walls hold you back. Through social media, your access to world-class teachers increases. Chat with educators all over the world. You can become as great as your drive allows you to be, so be a go-getter!

Revisit beginning-of-the-year procedures. Do this as often as needed. You all can become comfortable with each another and begin to get a little too lax with discipline. It's a good idea to cycle through procedures throughout the year as a refresher and a way to continue to hold students to a high standard.

Search for ideas in and out of the classroom. You might be a great teacher, but there is always something out there that could make you greater. Search for it and do not be fearful that looking for new ideas means you are less of a teacher. Some of your best ideas originate from another teacher, and you can tweak an idea to make it your own. Online resources are a huge hit—anything from teacher-created materials to blogs. Stay current by seeing what is out there and taking a risk by trying it out in your classroom. You're not going to be great at everything. An area that is your strength can be shared, and an area that is your weakness can be found elsewhere. There's no need to recreate the wheel.

Stay curious. Strive to be better so that you don't shortchange yourself or your students. Read books and scour the internet. Do whatever you can to remain inspired and learn about what you love to learn about. You'll be amazed at how something that you think is unrelated to teaching (like hiking, for instance) will come into play while teaching a lesson (maybe you refer to it in a Math problem or when introducing physical characteristics in Social Studies). Students love to see you get excited and share your interests, so fuel those interests as often as possible.

Stay involved in and around your school. When you partner with staff on different committees to serve the school, you learn a lot about the inner workings of effective relationships. Those same skills learned through various school activities can help you reach students in the classroom. Plus, students love to see your face outside of the classroom as you help out around the school. This sets a great example for your students on how to work as a team and take pride in a community.

Take risks repeatedly. Nothing is gained in remaining safe. To truly upgrade your effectiveness in the classroom, you need to challenge yourself to try new things over and over. If a strategy or approach doesn't work initially, try it again at a later date. There might have been a disconnect in subject area, student maturity, or overall organization. There will always be new students, new curriculum, or new situations you face as the years roll on, so do not rule out a strategy or approach because it didn't work well the first time you tried it.

Becoming a skilled educator requires constant reflection and ambition to constantly push the envelope. If you have reached this chapter, that means you have seen the fruits of your labor, from landing a job to becoming great at it. All of this time you have been focusing on yourself as you honed your craft. Take time now to pour into someone else. Your impact needs to go beyond your classroom walls, to impact students in other classrooms in your school, district, state, and beyond. Teaching is a selfless profession aimed at bettering others. Take all that you have learned and give back to your profession as a way to thank those who helped you develop your talents. May we all work together to make this world a better, brighter place.

About the Author

Gretchen Elizabeth Bridgers is an elementary educator in Charlotte, North Carolina. She has taught grades 2, 3 and 5 at both low and high performing public schools in a large district.

She is passionate about educating students through engaging, rigorous instruction where increased ownership develops student leaders.

Gretchen received her bachelor's degree at Marist College in Poughkeepsie, New York. Later, she received her master's degree in Curriculum and Supervision from the University of North Carolina at Charlotte. Finally, she obtained her National Board Certification as an Early Childhood Generalist.

With years under her belt mentoring new teachers, providing professional development to school building staff, and presenting at district and national conferences, Gretchen now invests her time solely into consulting individual teachers and school staff.

To book Gretchen for keynote speeches and professional development workshops, please email: gretchen@alwaysalesson.com.

You can also connect with Gretchen on various social media channels as *Always A Lesson*.

Made in the USA
Columbia, SC
28 September 2019